T0194338

THE WAY IS
Love

THE WAY IS Love

How to Walk in Love and Forgiveness

Errington D. Cumberbatch

THE WAY IS LOVE
HOW TO WALK IN LOVE AND FORGIVENESS

iUniverse books may be ordered through booksellers or by contacting:

iUniverse
1663 Liberty Drive
Bloomington, IN 47403
www.iuniverse.com
1-800-Authors (1-800-288-4677)

Because of the dynamic nature of the Internet, any web addresses or links contained in this book may have changed since publication and may no longer be valid. The views expressed in this work are solely those of the author and do not necessarily reflect the views of the publisher, and the publisher hereby disclaims any responsibility for them.

Any people depicted in stock imagery provided by Thinkstock are models, and such images are being used for illustrative purposes only. Certain stock imagery © Thinkstock.

ISBN: 978-1-4917-8885-1 (sc)
ISBN: 978-1-4917-8886-8 (e)

Library of Congress Control Number: 2016904670

Print information available on the last page.

iUniverse rev. date: 4/8/2016

If Jesus is the way
and Jesus is love
and the Bible is truth,
having the love of Jesus
in our hearts is the way
to abundant life
on earth, as it is in Heaven!

Love and Forgiveness Is the Way

Preparing for a Love and Forgiveness Experience and Expanding the Knowledge of God

That you may have a walk worthy of the Lord, fully pleasing Him, being fruitful in every good work and increasing in the knowledge of God. Strengthened with all might, according to His glorious power, for all patience and long-suffering with joy.
♥ Colossians 1:10–11 NKJV

In Memory of

Margaret Roberta McIntosh Cumberbatch,
my first love and my first wife,
who supported me during 35 years of marriage
and encouraged me to go to Canada Christian College.

Roberta went home to be with the
Lord in November 2008.

Yvonne Cumberbatch, my eldest daughter,
who went home to be with the Lord in November 2013.

To all of our children, grandchildren,
and great–grandchildren

We love you all.

Millions of people today are searching
for a reliable voice of authority.

The Word of God is the
only real authority.

Contents

i

Foreword

THE FUNDAMENTAL PRINCIPLES which underpin the Christian life are love and forgiveness. These quintessential qualities of our faith are summed up by God Himself who commands us to love Him first and then to love our neighbours as we would love ourselves.

The very first principles used by Almighty God in His work of redemption, reconciliation and restoration of man were love and forgiveness. It is therefore very obvious from this that there can be no redemption, reconciliation or no restoration without forgiveness – forgiveness is a main tributary of the river of love.

We have found ourselves rooted deeply in the mire of personal, social and environmental change. It seems people are suffering from fear, anxiety and hopelessness more than ever before in these changing times. High unemployment, family separations, teenage crime, violence and sexuality, absence of morals and spiritual values have all helped to create a selfish behaviour that is not very embracing. Hence the teaching of love and forgiveness in this time is so important.

From Matthew chapters five and six we understand that no one should think that he can receive anything from God if he entertains unforgiveness in his heart. We need to forgive to be forgiven, for love will cover a multitude of sins. The door to forgiveness always swings upon our own willingness to forgive those who have wronged us.

Pastor Cumberbatch has produced a solid biblical work on "love and forgiveness" that reminds us of our spiritual struggle in maintaining that right attitude and behaviour to each other. This book is written to all people in all cultures and for all times. The universality of the message is evident in the revelation of the limitless power that is inherent in the principle of love and forgiveness – a power that absolutely cancels the offence of others against you.

The lack of love and the spirit of unforgiveness unknowingly reveal and expose our own shortcomings. Those who submit to the power of unforgiveness must remember the words of the Apostle Paul in Romans 6:16 "Know you not that to whom you yield yourselves servants to obey, his servants you are...."

It is my personal belief that this book has the propensity to expose that ungodly spirit of unforgiveness and lack of love among believers and ignite a mighty deliverance across the Body of Christ in the nations. This will result in the restoration, refreshing and freedom among the brethren.

I unreservedly recommend that the foundational teaching on this very important subject matter be represented in churches across the nations and applied by every Kingdom citizen so that deliverance and total healing from every form of sickness in our body can be experienced.

Senator Rev Dr David Durant, J.P.
Senior Pastor
Restoration Ministries International
Gunsite Road, Brittons Hill
St. Michael
Barbados. West Indies

Pastor Errington Cumberbatch loves the Lord and has a heart for healing and deliverance. When he heard about the Health To You Ministry's *Walking In Wholeness Basic Course* he was eager to find out more about the ministry. He came to our course with a hunger for God and a desire to learn more about our Heavenly Father's love and this ministry of healing. Dr. Caroline Leaf says that when we live in love all of our body systems work perfectly.

Errington has an intimate relationship with his Heavenly Father, lives and walks in the Father's love and exemplifies it in his daily life. In 2011, Errington and his wife Jane, stepped out in faith and followed the call of God to bring this teaching to Barbados.

The topics in this book are key to living in wholeness and having healthy relationships. I bless you as you read and are transformed by the words of knowledge contained in *The Way Is Love.*

Errington is a man of integrity and rejoices in helping others come into a wonderful relationship of wholeness, first with God and then with others. He and his wife, Jane are an integral part of our Health To You Ministry team working in Barbados.

Rev J Timothy Roberts
Executive Director
Health To You Ministry (Canada)

Preface

WHEN I BEGAN TO WRITE this book, I was thinking about the world and what is happening to our society. I pondered in my heart some issues we are facing today. Is there an answer to these questions?

- Why is there so much hatred, discrimination, and racism in our world?
- How much better would our lives be if we just loved one another?
- Can man's intellectual advancement solve his social, cultural, and relational problems?
- Is it even possible for everyone to love each other?
- Why are there so many different religions?
- Are human beings important to God?
- Are there evil spirits around us?
- Why do curses run in some families?
- Can a Christian be demon-possessed?
- Do evil spirits affect Christians?

I am excited to think that the chapters in this book will have a positive effect and address some of these issues. I am sure that this book will open your mind, your eyes, your heart, and your spirit, so that you will not only know that the Holy Spirit is in you but will understand how to hear from God through the Holy Spirit.

I hope with all my heart that you will feel the love in this book, because my desire – and God's desire – is for you to have an abundant life. God created us, and we are so important to Him that He created us in His own image and likeness. He loves us so much that He gave His only begotten Son to suffer for our sins, die on the cross for our salvation, and rise again so that we can have eternal life. Jesus lives today.

It's not about religion – it's about a relationship with Jesus Christ, our Lord and Saviour and our Heavenly Father. God said, "I have loved you with an everlasting love; therefore, with loving kindness I have drawn you" (Jeremiah 31:3). We don't need more religion in this world; we need more Jesus. In spite of our intellectual advancement, we still cannot solve our social, cultural, and religious problems. One of the reasons, I believe, is that many people want to exclude God from everything. God created us; He wants us to worship Him. Without Him, we can do nothing.

Medical science is discovering that the Bible is truth. Medical science actually enhances the Bible and the Bible enhances medical science. Dr. Caroline Leaf is a Neuroscientist who has an amazing way of teaching both the scientific and spiritual aspects of the mind and the mind-body connection in easy to understand terms. In 2 Corinthians 10:5 Scripture tells us to take every thought captive, and I emphasize this throughout my teaching. Because of Dr. Leaf's book, *Who Switched Off My Brain*,

I can see and understand how science lines up with the effectiveness of the daily principles God has laid out for us in His Word. Medical science also validates that many diseases are stress-related and affected by our "*emotional* well-being". The *Merck Manual* references that approximately eighty percent of disease are "etiology unknown". If a disease is of an unknown or undetermined cause, the cause is most likely, *spiritual.* (Those that are stress-related also are spiritually-rooted.)

Even though God created us spirit, soul, and body as separate entities, we are intimately integrated. What happens in our body also affects our soul and spirit. Life is actually a spiritual force! The mind has the power of intellect, emotions, and free-will and, if enabled by the spirit and empowered by the Holy Spirit, can make good choices to positively change the body – which improves the brain.

Do you know that love is a spirit and that the same spirit of love can bring your body into alignment with the way God created it to be, establishing an atmosphere for healing? If we all loved one another, what do you think would happen to sickness and disease? And if we all had love in our hearts, would we be at war or even dealing with terrorism? A spirit of love changes our thought lives. If our thought lives are good, is there any room for evil, hatred, killing, or murder with the tongue?

Have you spent your life trying to meet the expectations of others? Perhaps from the time you were a child someone has forced you to take on a certain personality, job, or lifestyle. Are you the person today that God planned you to be? Do you know who you are? You can change your life with the power of love. It is life, and it is health. Keep going. The best is yet to come, because God has a plan for your life, and His plan is always perfect. It is God who writes the last chapter in the book of life.

Perhaps this book will answer some of the questions that we all have in these days and bring us one little step closer to global peace and harmony. In order to achieve this, we must walk in love and forgiveness and be obedient to God.

Love and blessings,

Errington D. Cumberbatch

Acknowledgements

I WAS ENCOURAGED BY THE Lord to write this book, and as I started to write, the Holy Spirit inspired me and gave me downloads to include in the book.

I want to thank my wife, Jane, for her support and assistance with the writing of this book. I love you.

A special thank-you goes to Dr Rondo Thomas, Professor and Vice President of Canada Christian College; and Dr Clarence Duff, Dean/Professor of Psychology and Counselling, Canada Christian College, for encouraging me to get started on this project when I had the vision.

I extend a very special thank-you to Rev Tim Roberts, Executive Director of Health To You Ministry in Canada, who has encouraged me, mentored me, and supported me as I took a step of faith to bring the Walking in Wholeness Course to Barbados, my country of birth.

Along this journey, several key leaders in Barbados have encouraged and endorsed the teaching of Walking In Wholeness Barbados Inc. They are Bishop Othneil Forde, Full Gospel Assembly; Rev Dr Holmes Williams, The Peoples' Cathedral; Rev Andre Symmonds, The Peoples' Cathedral; Bishop Justin McIntosh, Pentecostal Church of the Living God; Rev Lionel Gibson, Past Chairman, The

General Assembly of the Church of God; Senator Rev Dr David Durant, Restoration Ministries International; Rev Wendell Weekes, Church of God Greens; Rev Dr Michael Crichlow, Trinity Outreach Ministries International, Dr Orlando Seale, Church of the Nazarene, Pastor Eileen Rowe, Elim Pentecostal Temple; Pastor Victor Payne, Paynes Bay Pentecostal Church; and, Pastor Sherwood Howell, Six Men's Bay Pentecostal House of Prayer.

We also want to thank our Barbados Team for all their support and dedication to the Ministry of Walking In Wholeness Barbados Inc. They are: Margaret Caddle, Erlene Jordan, Pastor Jonlyn Harewood, Alston Larrier, Jacynthia Marquis, Isalene Riley, Deborah Ruck, Heather Ruck, Hilda Thompson, Carol Thorne, Matthew Thorne, and Rev Wendell Weekes.

It has been a personal journey and a learning experience. I thank all the people whom I have met along the way who have encouraged me.

The book reflects the real lives of people I have met through personal encounters – some of whom I met through the Walking in Wholeness Course, and some of whom I have counselled and helped to walk in the way of the Lord. I love each and every one of you unconditionally.

I pray this book will help people to be free and to know how to love and forgive others – and to walk in victory!

For they are life to those who find them, healing and health to all their flesh.

♥   Proverbs 4:22 NKJV

Introduction

THE PURPOSE OF THIS BOOK is to describe how God's Word and His creative power will work for you in your life, for the healing and transformation of your mind and body. As you apply these principles to your life and change your way of thinking, you will learn how to recognize good thoughts versus toxic thoughts and raise your level of discernment of the things around you. Are you aware that words can affect your life? God's Word is a creative power that will work for you, if released in faith and put into practice. You can speak things into existence, whether financial shortages or gains, sickness or health, failure or success. This book will challenge you to change how you speak and to choose faith-filled words. By speaking and confessing scripture daily, you will bring faith into your heart, and you will begin to see God's creative power to change the circumstances of your life.

God wants to be involved in your life, in your marriage, and in how you relate to others. God wants to be involved in your speech: in what you say and how you say it. This is very important to Him. God wants to be involved in your finances and in your health. God delights in your prosperity. He gives you power to secure wealth, that He may establish His covenant upon the earth (Deuteronomy 8:18; 11:12). God is interested in every little detail of your life.

Learn how to walk in love and forgiveness and how to program your spirit for success. Confess God's Word daily until the faith comes.

God will bestow His blessings upon you if you are obedient to His Word. He wants you to be blessed. Blessings will begin to appear in your life when you read the Word of God. Psalm 119:105 says, "Your Word is a lamp unto my feet and a light unto my path." God will lead us in the right direction. All blessings come from knowing God's Word and doing what He tells us. Our children also need to see the power of God working in our lives, so they can be witnesses to the darkness in the world. God still works in miracles today, even as He did in biblical days. The blessings that Abraham received also belong to you. God made a covenant to bless Abraham, his seed, and all the generations through him. He promised to make Abram a father of all nations, and He changed his name to Abraham, which means "Father of Nations" (Genesis 17-4-5). Because of this covenant, and by obeying God and His Word, you can receive the same blessings as Abraham did.

Much of the information contained in this book is from the Health To You Ministry course notes written by Rev J Timothy Roberts. This is the teaching ministry that God called us to bring to Barbados in 2011. *A More Excellent Way*, written by Henry W. Wright, is used as a reference regarding how illness can enter the body and the specific diseases that can result from sin. The scientific information about the brain and how our thoughts work come from books and emails from Dr Caroline Leaf, a Christian neuroscientist. Holy Spirit directed the writing and format of this book and the compilation of facts. These have been put together in an easy-to-read-and-understand format to help people learn how to walk in love and forgiveness. This is the key to walking in wholeness, which is God's way.

This book has been written with the guidance of the Holy Spirit and my experience in pastoral care, healing and deliverance. Much information is based on the *Walking In Wholeness Basic Course*, which is taught in Barbados under the direction of Pastor Tim Roberts, Executive Director of Walking in Wholeness Barbados Inc., a division of Health To You Ministry (Canada). My wife and I are both on the Board of Directors of Walking in Wholeness Barbados Inc. and we now reside in Barbados. Our goal is to build a Barbadian teaching team to take this ministry to the remainder of the Caribbean, as prophesied.

Be blessed, in Jesus's name.

Chapter One

THE PRIORITY OF

THE PRIORITY OF LOVE IS to challenge Christians – and non-Christians – to live victoriously, to grow spiritually, and to know God intimately, while proclaiming the truth and the power of the gospel of Jesus Christ with great enthusiasm and love.

Are you aware that love is a spirit given to us by God? The "spirit of love" that comes from God is different from the world's usual definition of love. When you have the spirit of love in you, your body will come into alignment with the way God created it to be, and this creates an atmosphere for healing. Are you aware that what happens in your body also affects your spirit and your soul? God created you spirit, soul (the mind, emotions, senses), and body. All three parts work together. What happens on one level affects the other two.

Life itself is actually a spiritual force. The mind has the power of intellect, emotions, and free will. If enabled by the spirit and empowered by the Holy Spirit, it can make choices that positively change the body, including the brain. Dr Caroline Leaf (a Christian neuroscientist) states that love changes the molecules in our brains, and when we are thankful, our brains release nerve growth factors that actually help change them. When we love God, we are thankful that He first loved us. Can a "spirit of love" change our thoughts? If our thoughts are focussed on things that are pure, there will be no room for evil, hatred, murder – or murder with the tongue. Everything we do begins with a thought, and the average person processes over 30,000 thoughts per day. It is very important to have loving thoughts.

Love is life! The love of God is already established in Heaven forever. When we walk in love, our bodies are healthy. That is why God tells us to love one another. Love covers a multitude of sins. If we are not walking in love, we are walking in fear, and fear is sin. Fear causes anxiety and stress, which will make us sick. Disease comes into our bodies through fear.

Forever, O Lord, Your word is settled in heaven [stands firm as the heavens].

♥ Psalm 119:89 AMP

Do you know there is such a thing as an "unloving spirit"? The unloving spirit is one of the most powerful and effective principalities working in the lives of mankind today. Unloving spirits put us down and cause us to fear men. When we are living in fear, we unknowingly give the enemy access to our bodies and minds. If we have love, we will have much brighter, healthier lifestyles – lives worth living!

For God did not give us a spirit of timidity or cowardice or fear, but [He has given us a spirit] of power and of love and of sound judgment and personal discipline [abilities that result in a calm, well–balanced mind and self-control].
♥ 2 Timothy 1:7 AMP

Think about this: If we all loved one another, what would happen to sickness and disease? What would happen to war? There would be no terrorists in the world, because there would be no hate. Let brotherly love continue, and remember to entertain strangers, for by so doing, some have unwittingly entertained angels.

Jesus said to him, "You shall love the Lord your God with all your heart, with all your soul, and with all your mind. This is the first and great commandment. And the second is like it: You shall love your neighbour as yourself. On these two commandments hang all the Law and the Prophets.
♥ Matthew 22:37–40 NKJV

God is love and He is spirit. His love is constant! People change, but God is the same yesterday, today, and forever. He loved us before we were born; He loves us today; He will love us forever. He never wavers. God's love is secure and unchangeable. He will never stop loving His believers. He gave His only begotten Son, Jesus Christ, so that we could have eternal life. That is love!

Love is universal. God made it that way! When we love unconditionally, in that context love is beautiful – the most beautiful thing. Love is a spirit. It is in us, and we have to work to maintain it, just as when we plant a garden. We have to take care of that garden by watering it, pulling out the weeds, and cultivating the ground. It is the same with love. If we realize how important love is, we won't have a desire to dislike, hate, mistreat, or abuse anyone – mentally, physically, or verbally.

Let's Understand Love

The Bible says that love will cover a multitude of sins. The reason is that no one can fight or argue with love. Jesus Christ *is* love. So, if Christ is in us, that same "agape" love will be in us as well. We need to nurture it, live it, and give it away to others. God loves us all, and He loves us unconditionally. Jesus said the greatest commandment is to love. This doesn't mean that *maybe* we should love. It means we *must* love. It is a command from God Himself, and we have to do it with joy in our hearts. This is the only way to experience true love, and it is opposite to the way the world demonstrates love.

Love is life! Money can't buy it. Love is a gift from God – He gave it to us. Let's not abuse it! Living in love will change our lives, and as we learn how important love is in our lives, we will have more abundance in our lives. The only part of life we can control is our reaction to it. If we choose to react to everything in love, our lives will be changed positively! We will be able to live our lives with joy in our hearts.

Scripture tells us to love our neighbours as ourselves. It is important to *love ourselves* first, so we are able to love others. Sometimes we find it difficult to love ourselves, and when we don't love ourselves, we open a door for the enemy (the devil or Satan) to come in. *Satan* means "adversary" or "accuser". Satan only comes to steal, kill, and destroy. Self-hatred is an opening for Satan and his diseases to take over our bodies. Self-hatred and guilt may even result in Alzheimer's disease. Alzheimer's disease, according to recent research in the medical community, seems to involve a proliferation of white corpuscles congregating at critical nerve junctions in the brain, or congregating in the brain and producing non-bacterial inflammation, interrupting nerve transmissions. Whenever white corpuscles are attacking the body and not doing what God created them to do, without exception, there will be various degrees of self-hatred and guilt. If we could stop the white corpuscles from collecting at critical nerve junctions of the brain, Alzheimer's might cease to exist (*Wright*, 260). This is just one example of how important it is for us to love one another and to love ourselves. God's Word is truth. He knows what He is talking about. He created us!

Love is very important.
It should take priority in our lives.

Scripture says that we are to love sincerely, hate what is evil, and turn away from wickedness. Let us hold fast to that which is good and let our love be without hypocrisy.

Important Principles to Consider

- Be kindly affectionate to one another, with brotherly love, in honour, giving preference to one another.
- Be diligent in serving the Lord and on fire with the spirit of God.
- Rejoice and delight in the hope we have in Christ.
- Be steadfast and patient in suffering and tribulation.
- Be constant in prayer.
- Share in the necessities of the saints (our brothers and sisters in Christ).
- Contribute to the needs of people.
- Always practice hospitality.

Can we learn to bless those who persecute us or who are cruel in their attitude towards us, instead of cursing them? Let's rejoice with those who rejoice and weep with those who weep, and let's be of the same mind toward each other, living in harmony with one another. Let us put away haughtiness and high-mindedness and readily adjust to people and things, giving ourselves to humble tasks. Let us not be wise in our own opinions or overestimate ourselves. (This doesn't mean to be a doormat, by any means.)

Be not wise in your own eyes; reverently fear and worship the Lord and turn [entirely] away from evil.
♥ Proverbs 3:7 AMP

Let's Look at the Word *Love*

L = Living Love

O = Obedience

V = Vital Importance

E = Energy

Living Love (God's Way)

If we live our lives with love in our hearts, we will receive all of God's blessings. If we live lives filled with love for God, ourselves, and others, there will be no room for hatred, anger, resentment, jealousy, bitterness, murder, or murder with the tongue. There will be peace in this world – the peace of God. The most beautiful thing we can do in life is to walk the path to holiness that God has set before each one of us. Through an act of our free will and with the love of God in our hearts, in cooperation with the Divine Will of God, we can become His instruments to accomplish His Will in the world. These days there is much talk about climate change and global warming. There is a climate change, but it has nothing to do with weather patterns. There is a climate of moral degeneration supported by politicians, mass media, and even the legal system itself. All of this is reflected in fashions, music, and entertainment. A whole generation has been compromised. There is a foul climate of compromise and confusion which is taking over the world. The spiritual climate change the world *needs* is love. When people live love God's way, it will change the climate of this world. It will change the atmosphere and bring the world into alignment with God's Divine Will. We must place Holy Love over us like an umbrella of protection, shielding us from the storm of compromise.

Obedience

Just as a servant knows that he must first obey his master in all things, so the surrender to an unquestionable obedience must become the essential characteristic of our lives. Deuteronomy 7:12–15 advises that if we are careful to obey the laws and live them, the Lord our God will keep His agreement of love with us. He promised this to our ancestors. He will love and bless us. He will bless our children. The Lord will take away all sickness from us. When we obey the Lord, He will love, bless, and multiply us. His blessings will overtake us. He will also bless the fruits of our bodies and the fruits of our land – our grain, our new wine, and our oil. Isn't that awesome? If I am obedient, I will be blessed in every area of my life – spiritually as well.

Vital Importance

The letter *V* is for "vital". All religions have some idea of the importance of love. Christian theology stresses the importance of love, because God has revealed that He is love (1 John 4:8,16). Love is both what God is and what He has done; God always acts in love. It is vitally important that we love the Lord our God with all our hearts, with all our souls (minds), and with all our strength (might), and that we love our neighbours as ourselves. In other words, we must love one another. Jesus said, "these words, which I command you today shall be in your minds and in your hearts." (Here, Jesus uses the word *heart* to refer to our *spirit* within us, not the organ that regulates the blood through our bodies.) He tells us to teach them diligently to our children and to talk about them when we sit in our houses, when we walk by the wayside, when we lie down, and when we rise up in the morning. "You shall bind them as a sign upon your hand and they shall be as frontlets [forehead bands] between your eyes. And you shall write them upon the door posts of your house and on your gates (Deuteronomy 6:1–9)." There is also a caution against disobedience here (Deuteronomy 6:10–25). It says in the Scriptures to be careful! Don't forget the Lord. Respect the Lord and serve only Him. Do not follow other gods. The Lord hates it when His people worship other gods! We must be sure to obey His commands and follow all the teachings and laws He has given us. We must do what is right and good and pleasing to the Lord, so everything will go well.

Energy

The letter *E* stands for "energy". Love has to be given away. If we have it and we don't give it away, we really don't have it. Love is a spirit. Scripture tells us that God did not give us a spirit of fear but of power, love, and a sound mind. We have to put energy into love. Our heavenly Father set the first example by giving us His only begotten son, Jesus Christ, who demonstrated it extremely well for us and set the example. He gave His life for us! We may never understand how big a price He paid. When Jesus was in the garden praying, he said, "Father, if it is Your will, remove this cup from Me; nevertheless, not My will but Yours be done." Scripture tells us that Jesus was using up a lot of energy and an angel appeared to Him from heaven to strengthen Him. The Scriptures also tell us that He was in agony as He prayed more earnestly, and his sweat became like great drops of blood (that is energy), because He loved us so much. If we, here on this earth, could only understand this and comprehend what a sacrifice this was and understand that He did it for us. We need to discard selfishness and self-centredness. We must repent and move forward with the love of Jesus in our hearts.

When we are born-again Christians, we can have that same agape love that our Heavenly Father and our Lord and Saviour, Jesus Christ, have, because Christ is in us, and we are in Him. Man is created in the image of God. God has given us a heart to love like He loves and to bless others with His compassion. Angels look in with wonder at the gift God has given to man. Scripture tells us that we should strive to be more like Jesus, which means that we can have that agape love in us to share with everyone. Jesus said not to call Him Lord if we were not going to do what He said. We would be wasting our time and putting a hindrance in our prayer life. He cautioned against disobedience. Disobedience is like witchcraft, which is sin. No one can enter the Kingdom of Heaven when dealing in witchcraft (Deuteronomy 28: 15–68).

For God's wrath; for it is written, vengeance is mine.

Vengeance is Mine, and retribution, in due time their foot will slip; for the day of their disaster is at hand, and their doom hurries to meet them.

♥ Deuteronomy 32:35 AMP

Repay no one evil for evil. Think on good things that are honest and proper and noble, living in peace with everyone. Do not seek revenge; instead, allow God to make sure justice is served. Turn it over to Him.

Beloved, never avenge yourselves, but leave the way open for God's wrath [and His judicial righteousness]; for it is written [in Scripture], "Vengeance is Mine, I will repay," says the Lord.

♥ Romans 12:19 AMP

Cathy: Anger and Retaliation

Cathy came to see us with anger in her heart towards her boyfriend. He had been treating her poorly, and one day they had words, and he did an evil thing to her. She left very upset and full of jealousy and anger. As she was leaving, she turned around, picked up a rock, and threw it at him. She missed but damaged the door to his house. Her boyfriend took the case to court, and she was ordered to pay damages for the door. She knew that the boyfriend had no intention of replacing the door, as the damage wasn't so great that it could not be repaired and still function for its purpose. She knew that he was just doing it for the money and to cause her more grief. God says, "Repay no one evil for evil", but this is what Cathy's first reaction was, and she acted on it. Cathy repented for retaliation and forgave her now ex-boyfriend for what he did. Cathy understood that what she had done was wrong and did what she had to do to make things right.

"'I will repay,' says the Lord; 'but if your enemy is hungry, feed him; if he is thirsty, give him a drink; for by doing so you will heap burning coals of fire upon his head. Do not let yourself be overcome by evil, but overcome evil with good' (Romans 12:1–21)." The importance of love is to make it a priority in our lives always. For love will cover a multitude of sins.

Above all, have fervent and unfailing love for one another, because love covers a multitude of sins [it overlooks unkindness and unselfishly seeks the best for others].

♥ 1 Peter 4:8 AMP

So he answered and said, "You shall love the Lord your God with all your heart, with all your soul, with all your strength, and with all your mind, and your neighbour as yourself."

♥ Luke 10:27 NKJV

Love is very important. The word *love* appears in the Bible 500 times. Jesus said you must have love to inherit eternal life. We must have love so we will live. The following key Scriptures talk about love:

Psalm 145:20	*The Lord preserves all who love him, but all the wicked He will destroy.*
Proverbs 10:12	*Hatred stirs up strife, but love covers all sins.*
Song of Solomon 1:2	*For your love is better than wine.*
Song of Solomon 2:4	*And His banner over me was love.*
Song of Solomon 3:5	*Do not stir up nor awaken love until it pleases.*
Song of Solomon 7:12	*Whether the grape blossoms are open, and the pomegranates are in bloom. There I will give you my love.*
Song of Solomon 8:6	*For love is as strong as death.*
Song of Solomon 8:7	*Many waters cannot quench love. Nor can the floods drown it.*
Romans 5:5	*Now hope does not disappoint, because the love of God has been poured out in our hearts by the Holy Spirit who was given to us.*
Romans 12:9	*Let love be without hypocrisy.*
Romans 13:8	*Owe no one anything, except love one another, for he who loves another has fulfilled the law.*
Romans 13:10	*Love does no harm to a neighbour [anyone]; therefore love is the fulfilment of the law.*
1 Corinthians 8:1	*Knowledge puffs up, but love edifies.*
1 Corinthians 13:4	*Love suffers long and is kind, love does not envy. Love does not parade itself, it is not puffed up.*
1 Corinthians 13:8	*Love never fails.*
1 Corinthians 13:13	*And now abide faith, hope, love, these three; but the greatest of these is love.*
1 Corinthians 13:5	*It is not rude; it is not self-seeking, it is not provoked [nor overly sensitive and easily angered]; it does not take into account a wrong endured.*

Galatians 5:22	But the fruit of the spirit is love, joy, peace, long-suffering, kindness, goodness, faithfulness, gentleness, self-control. Against such there is no law
Ephesians 5:25	Husbands, love your wives.
Colossians 3:19	Love your wives and do not be bitter toward them.
1 Timothy 1:5	Now the purpose of the commandments is love from a pure heart, from a good conscience; and from sincere faith.
1 Timothy 2:15	Nevertheless she will be saved in childbearing if they continue in faith, love, and holiness, with self-control.
1 Timothy 4:12	But be an example to the believers in word, in conduct, in love, in spirit, in faith, in purity.
Titus 2:4	Love their husbands.
Hebrews 13:1	Let brotherly love continue.
1 Peter 2:17	Love the brotherhood.
1 Peter 5:14	Greet one another with kiss of love.
1 Peter 3:8	Finally, all of you be of one mind, having compassion for one another; love as brothers, be tender-hearted, be courteous.
1 Peter 3:10	For he who would love life; and see good days, let him refrain his tongue from evil, and his lips from speaking deceit.
2 Peter 1:7	To godliness brotherly kindness, and to brotherly kindness love.
1 John 4:7	Beloved, let us love one another, for love is of God; and everyone who LOVES is born of God and knows God.
1 John 4:8	He who does not love does not know God, for God is love.
Proverbs 16:24	Pleasant words are like a honeycomb. Sweetness to the soul and health to the bones.

God loves you, and so do I.
Let's love one another.

The cross itself symbolizes this relationship of love. Like the vertical post of the cross, our lives must receive the love of God from above, and with outstretched arms in a horizontal position, we can extend this love to others. As God loves us, so we should love each other.

Through the cross,
Jesus declared His love for all.

Chapter Two

MY DADDY LOVES ME

THE HEART OF OUR HEAVENLY Father is love. He loves us more than we can ever imagine. He created us because He wants to have a loving relationship with us. We can never compare the love of our Heavenly Daddy with our earthly dads.

> *Behold what manner of love the Father has bestowed*
> *on us, that we should be called children of God!*
> ♥ 1 John 3:1 NKJV

We are children of God! The Father loves us! John tells us that the Father has "lavished" His love on us, which portrays an action and the extent of God's love. As children of God, we have a loving relationship with our Heavenly Father. God's fatherhood is eternal. He is eternally the Father of Jesus Christ, and through Jesus He is our Father. Through Jesus we receive the Father's love and are called "children of God".

Agape Love

It is so important to understand that our Heavenly Father loves us very much, with an agape love. *Agape* is a Greek word often translated as "love" in the New Testament. How is "agape love" different from other types of love? The essence of agape love is self-sacrifice. Agape love is unique and is distinguished by its nature and character. Agape is love which is of and from God, whose very nature is love itself. The apostle John affirms this in 1 John 4:8: "God is love." God does not merely love; He *is* love itself. Everything God does flows from His love. But it is important to know that God's love is not a sappy, sentimental love such as we often hear portrayed. God loves because that is His nature and the expression of His being. He loves the unlovable and the unlovely (us), not because we deserve to be loved, but because it is His nature to love us, and He must be true to His nature and character.

God's love is displayed most clearly at the cross, where Christ died for the unworthy creatures who were "dead in trespasses and sins" (Ephesians 2:1) – not because we did anything to deserve it. But God shows and proves His love toward us in that while we were yet sinners Christ died for us (Romans 5:8). There is nothing we can do to merit God's love. We are the undeserving recipients upon whom He "lavishes" that love. His love was demonstrated when He sent His Son into the world to seek and save the lost, (Luke 19:10) and to provide eternal life to those He sought and saved. He paid the ultimate sacrifice for those He loves.

In the same way, we are to love others sacrificially. Jesus gave the parable of the good Samaritan as an example of sacrifice for the sake of others – even those who may care nothing at all for us or even hate us, as the Jews did the Samaritans. Sacrificial love is not based on a feeling but a determined act of the will, a joyful resolve to put the welfare of others above our own. This type of love does not come naturally to humans because of our fallen nature. We are incapable of producing such a love. If we are to love as God loves, with that agape love, it can only come from its true source, the Father. This is the love which has been poured out in our hearts through the Holy Spirit and given to us when we became His children (Romans 5:5). Now that love is in our hearts, so we can obey Jesus, who said,

A new commandment I give to you, that you love one another; as I have loved you, that you also love one another.

♥ John 13:34 AMP

This new commandment involves loving one another as He loved us, sacrificially, even to the point of death. It is clear that only God can generate within us the kind of self-sacrificing love which is the proof that we are His children. Because of God's love toward us, we are now able to love one another.

By this we know the love, because He laid down His life for us. And we also ought to lay down our lives for the brethren.

♥ 1 John 3:16 NKJV

Scripture makes it very clear that those who take their nature from God are His children, and those who take their nature from the devil are the devil's children.

In this the children of God and the children of the devil are manifest: Whoever does not practice righteousness is not of God, nor is he who does not love his brother. For this is the message that you heard from the beginning, that we should love one another.

♥ 1 John 3:10–11 NKJV

The Imperative of Love

The imperative of love is to practice righteousness and conform to God's will in purpose, thought, word, and action. We are of God. If we do not love our brothers (our fellow believers in Christ), we are not of God, and God will consider us as murderers, and we will not enter the Kingdom of Heaven. For this is the message which you have heard from the beginning, that we should love one another. All Christians should love one another, according to Scripture (1 John 3:10–11). If we don't, we are in disobedience to God and His Word. The Bible says that disobedience is like witchcraft, and witchcraft is sin. The blessings come when we walk in obedience to God. Deuteronomy 28:1–16 lists all the blessings. These blessings are for us today. The Lord says He is the same yesterday, today, and forever. He does not change (Malachi 3:6).

To the elect lady and her children, whom I love in truth, and not only I, but also all those who have known the truth, And now I plead with you, lady, not as though I wrote a new commandment to you, but that which we have had from the beginning: that we love one another. This is love, that we walk according to His commandments. This is the commandment, that as you have heard from the beginning, you should walk in it.
♥ 2 John 1:1, 5, 6 NKJV

Jesus instructs us to call God our Father when we pray (Luke 11:2). When we do this, it shows we are in His family. When we speak of God, we refer to the Godhead (Acts 17:29). The Godhead includes the Father, the living Word (who is Jesus), and the Holy Spirit (Genesis 1:1–2). The Father decrees, Jesus declares, and the Holy Spirit makes it happen.

> *But as many as received Him, to them He gave the right to become children of God, to those who believe in His name; who were born, not of blood, nor of the will of the flesh, nor of the will of man, but of God.*
>
> ♥ John 1:12–13 NKJV

Jesus also said that there is another spiritual father, who is the devil. The enemy tries his best to separate us from the Godhead. He wants to break up all other relationships we have, with ourselves and with others. Jesus said, in John 8:44, that there are two spiritual fathers in the world. One is His Father, God (Adonai), and the other is Satan, the devil (father of lies).

> *You are of your father the devil, and it is your will to practice the desires [which are characteristic] of your father. He was a murderer from the beginning, and does not stand in the truth because there is no truth in him. When he lies, he speaks what it natural to him, for he is a liar and the father of lies and half-truths.*
>
> ♥ John 8:44 AMP

Which father is yours? Let's make sure we belong to God's family. We are joint heirs, adopted into His family. He loves us so much! He cares about the little things. He listens to what we have to say.

> *For you did not receive the spirit of bondage again to fear, but you received the spirit of adoption by who we cry out, "Abba Father". The Spirit Himself bears witness with our spirit that we are children of God, and if children, then heirs – heirs of God and joint heirs with Christ, if indeed we suffer with Him, that we may also be glorified together.*
> ♥ Romans 8:15–17 NKJV

When Jesus was talking to the young believers, they were trying to claim, "We are sons of Abraham, and we are people of faith", but they had a huge "religious spirit". Religious spirits have no authority in Jesus Christ. Jesus hated religious spirits. Jesus was not a religious person. He did things that shook the religious kingdoms of the earth.

God the Father, through Jesus Christ, created us all. Let's make sure we are in God's family. When we are separated from God the Father, the curses that come into our lives include solitude, lack of purpose in life, many different diseases, and even death. We may not have a good understanding or a clear picture of our Heavenly Father, because our perception of a father may be based on our relationships with our earthly fathers. We may think our Heavenly Father is like our earthly dads. We cannot compare our earthly fathers with our Heavenly Father, because our earthly fathers may not understand how to love us. They may love us *conditionally*, not knowing that they are doing something wrong. What is the difference? Our Father, God, will love us unconditionally. His arms are always open to receive us and forgive us. He wants to have a personal relationship with each of us. He promises that He will never leave us nor forsake us. He wants the very best for us and for our lives.

One of the goals of the devil is to break up the family, because the family is ordained by God.

John Didn't Feel Loved by his Mother

John was referred to me because he was suicidal. He had two young sons and was sharing the responsibility of bringing them up with their mother, although they did not live together. When John came to see me, he was unemployed and very depressed. We dealt with some issues in his life, but when I spoke to him about his mother, his face changed. I knew immediately that there was something going on there. I called my wife over to stand in proxy for his mother. She simply took his hands in hers, looked him in the eyes, and said the following: "I stand in proxy for your mom. Whether your mom didn't know how to show love to you, or if she wasn't able to say she loves you, I have some healing words for your heart: I'm glad you were born. You were a good son. I love you. Will you please forgive me?" Jane offered John a hug, and John put his head on my wife's shoulder and cried for about five minutes. After the hug, his whole countenance changed, and I was able to work with him through some other issues in his life. John is now working in construction and going to university. His two sons are happy to have their father back, and John is a totally different person. That was a few years ago now, and each time I see John, he has something positive to tell us about his life and how things are going now. We give God all the glory and all the praise for working through us to help John get the freedom and transform his life.

Let's get to know the Godhead. Deuteronomy 6:4 says that Our God (Echad, which means plural unity) is one.

God said, let us (Father, Son, and Holy Spirit) make mankind in our image, after Our likeness …
♥ Genesis 1:26 AMP

I and the Father are one.
♥ John 10:30 AMP

And because you (really) are His Sons, God has sent the Holy Spirit of His Son into our hearts, crying, Abba (Father).
♥ Galatians 4:6 AMP

In Isaiah 48:16, and John 17:18, we have parallel statements: The Lord GOD (Adonai/God the Father) and His spirit have sent me. Then God (Jehovah Elohim) sends us into the world in the power of the Holy Spirit.

But you shall receive power when the Holy Spirit has come upon you; and you shall be witnesses to me, in Jerusalem, and in all Judea and Samaria, and to the end of the earth.
♥ Acts 1:8 NKJV

There is unity between the three persons of the Godhead who is one being. God the Father fathered his only begotten Son through the Holy Spirit, and we are born again into God's family and adopted by the same spirit. We are also one being, one person, in three parts – spirit, soul, and body. It is the character of fathers to "father" their children. God, the Father "fathered" His only begotten Son. Jesus Christ was not created! Now that same Heavenly Father wants us to be His children through the "new birth".

The Holy Spirit

> *Then the angel said to Mary, "The Holy Spirit will come upon you, and the power of God will overshadow you like a shining cloud; and so the holy, pure, sinless thing (offspring) which shall be born of you will be called the Son of God."*
> ♥ Luke 1:35 AMP

> *The wind blows (breathes) where it wills; and though you hear its sound, yet you neither know where it comes from nor where it is going. So it is with everyone who is born of the Holy Spirit.*
> ♥ John 3:8 AMP

In these Scriptures, we see that both Jesus's birth and the new birth of believers involve the Holy Spirit. When the first Christians received the Holy Spirit, as recorded in Acts 2:2–4, the Holy Spirit came with the rushing sound of the wind. As Jesus said, we do not always know when, and how, the Spirit of God comes into our lives, any more than we can see the wind. God's presence may come to us suddenly, like the rushing of the wind. Sometimes God's Spirit comes to us quietly, like a cool, soft breeze. Throughout our lives, we must be aware of God's Spirit and always welcome Him. People will see and hear God's Spirit as they watch His effects in their lives. Like the winds of Jerusalem, the Spirit of God can come to people in many ways, yet the effects are the same – it's a new birth. The wonderful thing about Pentecost was not so much the rushing, mighty wind or the tongues of fire but the disciples being filled with the Holy Spirit, that they might be witnesses to all people. If we do not have the desire to tell others of Jesus Christ, it is evident that we do not know the fullness of the Holy Spirit.

Heavenly Father vs. Earthly Dad

Most of us know someone with a broken heart. A broken heart is a broken spirit, and what affects the spirit also affects the soul and the body. That's why we see people looking for love in all the wrong places, walking around disillusioned; or some people may develop different personalities. They can turn into people-pleasers, or they may even look for acceptance by the way they perform. Many times they build walls around their hearts so no one can hurt them anymore. We probably all know someone like that. Many times this key person in their life is their dad or mom, who failed them. But here is good news! In our Heavenly Father's unconditional love, He is content just to be with us, to hang out with us, even if we don't do anything in particular. He longs to be in a relationship with us. An earthly father may make a deal with his son or daughter. He might say something like, "If you do well on your report card this term, I will buy you a new bike." Our Heavenly Daddy loves us no matter how well we perform and no matter what we do!

He loves us unconditionally.
He is always there for us!
We are His children.

Our Heavenly Dad is different from our earthly dad. We can't compare the two. Our earthly dads are human, and they make mistakes. Our Heavenly Dad is spirit, and He is love! Many of us could not share our thoughts, concerns, or frustrations; nor could we express our anger at a situation with our earthly dad, so we end up holding it all inside. With our Heavenly Dad, we can share anything – and everything – at any time. He won't be upset or angry. Our Heavenly Father will delight in our honesty. He loves taking note of even the smallest details of our lives, and He never changes. Psalm139: God's perfect knowledge of man. Matthew 6:25–34: Do good, please God, and don't worry. In James 1:17: Every good gift, and every perfect gift, comes from our Heavenly Daddy. Philippians 4:6–8: Be anxious for nothing, but in everything, by prayer and supplication, and with thanksgiving talk to our Heavenly Father. In other words, always pray and give Him thanks for everything, and in every circumstance, because He will help us through any situation. We can always go to Him with our problems. According to Psalm 68:5 and James 1:27, if our earthly dad is not being a father to us, we can always go to God, our Heavenly Daddy.

This is the message [of God's promised revelation] which we have heard from Him and now announce to you, that God is Light [He is holy, His message is truthful, He is perfect in righteousness], and in Him there is no darkness at all [no sin, no wickedness, no imperfection].

♥ 1 John 1:5 AMP

We are valued in the Father's heart, and He seeks those who would worship Him. We were created to worship God. He desires to have a close relationship with us. God is a spiritual being, and those who worship Him must worship Him in spirit and in truth (John 4:23). He has chosen us and ordained us to go forth and bear fruit, and our fruit should remain, so that whatever we ask of the Father in Jesus's name, He will give it to us. For the Father has no pleasure when someone dies. Choose life!

You did not choose Me, but I chose you and appointed you that you should go and bear fruit, and that your fruit should remain, that whatever you ask the Father in My name He may give you.

♥ John 15:16 NKJV

I call heaven and earth as witnesses today against you, that I have set before you life and death, blessing and cursing; therefore choose life, that both you and your descendants may live.
♥ Deuteronomy 30:19 NKJV

Psalm 139:13–14 says we are fearfully and wonderfully made. Jesus said, "I pray for them now. I am not praying for the people in the world, but I am praying for these people You gave me, because they are Yours. All I have is Yours, and all You have is Mine, and My glory is seen in them. Now I am coming to you. I will not stay in the world, but these followers of Mine are still in the world. Holy Father, keep them safe by the power of Your Name—the Name You gave me. They will be one, just as You and I are one." Our Heavenly Father wants us to be one with Him. His love is unconditional, and He wants us to be close to Him and draw near to Him.

I pray for them. I do not pray for the world but for those whom You have given Me, for they are Yours.
♥ John 17:9 NKJV

Now I am no longer in the world, but these are in the world, and I come to You. Holy Father, keep through Your name those whom You have given Me, that they may be one as We are.
♥ John 17:11 NKJV

There is nothing we can do that will make our Heavenly Daddy love us any less. God showed us His love through

Jesus. He will never leave us nor forsake us. Will you choose to live in that love? There is nothing we can do that will prevent God from loving us. Our Heavenly Father will always finish what He started (Philippians 1:6). After all, He is our sovereign, eternal, almighty God. How many projects do we humans start and never finish? Our Heavenly Daddy brings everything to completion.

Jesus gave us an example of how to pray, in the Lord's Prayer (Matthew 6:9–13). We can come to the Father with confidence. (See Hebrews 10:17–22; Luke 11:1–2; John 16:23–27 and Hebrews 11:6.) Our Heavenly Father loves us. He *is* love (Ephesians 2:4; 1 John 4:7–11). Nothing can separate us from His love (Romans 8:38,39). Jesus is the way, the truth, and the life. Jesus is the *only way* to the Father (John 14:6–9). God the Father spoke from the Heavens two out of three times, saying, "This is my beloved Son in whom I am well pleased" (Matthew 3:17).

He gave His only begotten Son for us.
He has a plan and purpose for our lives!

In Isaiah 53, our Heavenly Father was so full of pleasure in His heart, and the thought of having us in His family, that He was willing to judge Jesus, kill His only begotten Son, and raise Him from the dead. *Wow!* He decreed it as so! The joy of having us back in His family was greater than the pain of judging His Son. Can we ever doubt the love of God?

He knows everything about you.

He enjoys hangin' out with you.

He created you!

In James 1:17, we learn that only good and perfect gifts come from our Heavenly Father, who never changes. Anything unclean, unhealthy, or just not good for us comes from the evil kingdom. In Acts 2:22, and Acts 4:30, we learn that the Father gave the Holy Spirit to Jesus Christ, who gave it to us.

We must love and walk in forgiveness.

They go hand in hand.

When we walk through snow on a sunny day, we know we need our sunglasses along with our coat because the reflection of the sun on the snow is blinding. Underneath the snow there may be grass, dirt, stones, etc. The snow covers up what is underneath (covered under the blood of Jesus) and makes everything white by the dazzling blanket of snow. That is a picture of our Heavenly Daddy's forgiveness. Two verses in Scripture talk about how His love covers a multitude of sins (1 Peter 4:8 and James 5:20). The blood of Christ cleanses us from all sin, covers all our failures, and washes us whiter than snow. As children of God, that's how we should feel today – whiter than snow.

Purge me with hyssop, and I shall be clean; wash me, and I shall be whiter than snow.

♥ Psalm 51:7 NKJV

The Bible clearly says, "All have sinned" (Romans 3:23). The first sign that you need salvation is thinking, "That's for others, not me." If you haven't given your life to our Lord and Saviour Jesus Christ, I encourage you to ask Jesus into your heart. Pray the salvation prayer. Read it out loud so you can hear it, mean it with all your heart, and you will be saved. Hallelujah – praise the Lord!

Salvation Prayer (or Sinner's Prayer)

Dear God in heaven, I come to you in the name of Jesus. I acknowledge to You that I am a sinner, and I am sorry for my sins and the life that I have lived. I need your forgiveness.

I believe that your only begotten Son, Jesus Christ, shed His precious blood on the cross at Calvary and died for my sins, and I am now willing to turn from my sin.

You said in Your Holy Word, Romans 10:9, that if we confess to the Lord our God, and believe in our hearts that God raised Jesus from the dead, we shall be saved.

Right now I confess Jesus as the Lord of my soul. With my heart, I believe that God raised Jesus from the dead. This very moment I accept

*Jesus Christ as my own personal Saviour, and
according to His Word, right now, I am saved.*

*Thank you, Jesus, for your unlimited grace,
which has saved me from my sins. I thank you,
Jesus, that your grace never leads to license but
rather it always leads to repentance. Therefore,
Lord Jesus, transform my life so that I may bring
glory and honour to you alone and not to myself.
Thank you, Jesus, for dying on the cross for me
and giving me eternal life. Amen.*

When we come to Jesus, we realize that the most
important thing cannot be earned; the greatest gift can
never be repaid. The truth is that nothing we do can add to,
or take away from, the gift of salvation and a relationship
with our Heavenly Father. This is a difficult concept to
grasp in our culture of self-sufficiency. Accepting this gift
opens our hearts to God. As we meditate on His gentle
kindness and mercy, in the life and sacrifice of Christ, our
thankfulness grows; and we are filled with joy (Ephesians
2:1–10).

*For You formed my innermost parts; You knit me
[together] in my mother's womb. I will give thanks
and praise to You, for I am fearfully and wonderfully
made; wonderful are Your works, and my soul
knows it very well.*

♥ Psalm 139:13–14 AMP

Judgement

The Church (born–again Christians) will appear before the judgment seat of Christ, not the Father (Daniel 7:9; 2 Corinthians 5:10; Matthew 7:21–23; Revelation 20:11–15). It makes sense that the very one who gave His life so that we may have eternal life would be the one to whom we give account. Nothing can separate us (His children) from our Holy Father's love. We will not be judged by the Father, because the Father judged Jesus in our place. The Ancient of Days (the Father) will preside on the great white throne over the second death. The second death is mentioned several times in the book of Revelation and is synonymous with the lake of fire. It is a "death" in that it is a separation from God, the Giver of life. It is called "second" death because it follows physical death.

Most assuredly, I say to you, he who hears My word and believes in Him who sent Me has everlasting life, and shall not come into condemnation, but has passed from death into life.
♥ John 5:24 NKJV

There is, therefore, now no condemnation to those who are in Christ Jesus, who do not walk according to the flesh, but according to the Spirit.
♥ Romans 8:1 NKJV

Some Things to Consider and Do

1. Are you willing to, and/or will you choose to, forgive your earthly father and/or mother for breaking your heart or disappointing you, in whatever way it applies to your life? Do you choose to forgive him/her for not showing or expressing love toward you in word and deed, whether he/she would not, could not, or did not know how? Earthly dads or moms can only do what they know how to do, whether right or wrong. Can you choose to forgive your earthly dad and/or mom right now, knowing that they only did what they knew or understood?

2. Do you make a choice to accept and embrace God the Father's unconditional love for you? Do you accept your Heavenly Daddy (Abba) for who He is, and love Him for who He is (Romans 8:15)?

3. Identify Scripture verses that speak to your heart. Meditate on them and memorize them.

Behold what manner of love the Father has bestowed on us that we should be called children of God.
♥ 1 John 3:1 NKJV

It might be helpful to take a piece of paper and make two columns. In the left column write out in point form a descriptive list of what characterizes your earthly dad.

Opposite each point in the right column, write down the corresponding characteristic of our Heavenly Father.

EARTHLY FATHER	HEAVENLY FATHER
– not around much	– always with me
– provides what he can	– promises to supply all my needs
– often lies to cover his mistakes	–speaks the honest truth in love
– spends time with me sometimes	– loves to hang out with me

After doing this exercise, give thanks for who our Heavenly Father is. Review our Heavenly Father's traits frequently as a reminder. Give thanks for the good things God has brought into your life through your earthly dad, and pray for him in the areas where he may be lacking or need improvement. Have this same attitude with your mom. Forgive your earthly dad and/or mom for mistakes or choices they made, and understand that they only did what they knew how to do. Enjoy our Heavenly Dad to the fullest, living in His love, and bless your parents from the overflow of God's love.

Our Heavenly Father is different
from our earthly fathers!

Chapter Three

WHO BROKE
YOUR HEART?

THE "UNLOVING SPIRIT" IS ONE of the most powerful and controlling principalities working in the lives of mankind since the Garden of Eden. Lucifer (the devil or Satan) rebelled against God, and Adam and Eve agreed with him. Unloving spirits come out of bitterness, accusation, envy, jealousy, and rejection. If we have unloving spirits, we may have fear of other people. When we believe these anti-Christ spirits, we may begin to hate ourselves, and we may hide inside ourselves out of fear of what others might think or accept. Some people cut themselves or have suicidal thoughts. In 2 Timothy 3, we see how unloving spirits work in people's lives.

I didn't know about the unloving spirit until I took Health To You Ministry's *Walking In Wholeness Basic Course*. It was never mentioned to me in church. We may have this spirit in us and not know it, or like myself, not even know such a thing exists or that it may be affecting our lives. I want to shed some light in the darkness around the unloving spirit.

> *I will praise You, for I am fearfully and wonderfully made; marvellous are Your works, and that my soul knows very well. My frame was not hidden from You when I was made in secret, and skillfully wrought in the lowest parts of the earth. Your eyes saw my substance, being yet unformed, and in Your book they all were written, the days fashioned for me, when as yet there were none of them.*
> ♥ Psalm 139:14–16 NKJV

God says we were uniquely knit together in our mother's womb by God, our Creator. We are wonderfully made. He loves us just the way He made us! When we have an unloving spirit, we may dislike ourselves and worry about what others think about us. We may think everyone is looking at us and criticizing us. We may think we are not dressed as nicely or are not as smart as others. If we have an unloving spirit working in our lives, we may feel hated or rejected by ourselves or others. At some point in our lives, people may have said things like this:

- I wish you'd never been born.
- You were an accident.
- You weren't planned for.
- You messed up our lives. It's all your fault.
- Can't you ever do anything right?
- You'll never amount to anything.

These things may have been spoken over us when we were young, or even still in the womb, and the devil has trained our brains so that we now think it is true, and those thoughts keep repeating themselves over and over again in our minds.

If we have an unloving spirit, we may feel like garbage, unworthy, alone. Maybe we don't like the sound of our own voice and don't like what we see in the mirror. We may find it hard to look someone in the eye. Unloving spirits don't allow us to accept a compliment, so we will tend to say things like, "Oh, it was nothing," instead of receiving the compliment and saying thank you. We may even establish a wrong identity or put on a false face. When we go out in public, we may put on happy faces, but inside we are feeling sad and dark.

When we don't feel good about ourselves, we may tend to treat others poorly. We may even think that God will heal other people, but when it comes to ourselves, we think that we aren't good enough or worthy to be healed. When we read the Word of God, we may feel accused or think that God is picking apart our own personal traits. We may feel that what God says can't be true for us. We may often spend money on things we don't need to make ourselves feel better – a temporary lift. Some people may try to hurt themselves, eat too much, steal things, and/or use bad language. Are you aware that most people with addictions have an unloving spirit?

Traits of an Unloving Spirit

- *Feeling hated and/or rejected by ourselves or others.* Thinking we aren't liked. Believing things people have said to us that were not nice or maybe even condemning.

- *Feeling unclean or like garbage, unworthy, unlovely.* Believing accusatory or hurtful remarks made about us even by well-meaning people.
- *Not liking the sound of our own voices.* Not liking what we see in the mirror and maybe even shrinking away when saying our own names. Believing the lies of Satan and comparing ourselves to others we may envy, thinking they are better than we are.
- *Feeling separated from God, ourselves, and others.* Feeling lonely and perhaps as if life has no purpose; always looking for approval or for a compliment.
- *Being unable to look someone in the eye.* Unloving spirits take away our confidence and our sense of self-worth. We may feel ashamed of ourselves.
- *Being unable to accept a compliment.* If someone says something nice to us, we may contradict them. This is also a "victim spirit". We don't believe we are worthy, or we may even think that people are just saying it to be nice.
- *Using a false identity.* How we feel about ourselves may be based on rejection, self-bitterness, envy, self-hate, etc. God created us, and He said we were "very good"! Don't you think that if we don't believe we are "very good", then we are saying our Heavenly Daddy made a mistake?
- *Treating others poorly.* We tend to put other people down, even if we do it by using words of love. This makes people think that we don't love them.

- *Believing others will be healed* but thinking that we are not good enough for God to heal us!
- *Feeling accused.* Even when we read God's Word, we feel as if He is accusing us. We take innocent comments made by others the wrong way.
- *Thinking it can't be true for us.* Even though God says we are beloved children, we may believe that doesn't include *us*. When we do this, we are actually going against God and His Word. We might think that no one loves us, so why should God love us?
- *Come against yourself.* We may try to hurt ourselves. Some people cut themselves. We may spend money on things we don't need or eat more than we should. Some people want to steal things from stores, and others use foul language.

Who broke your heart?
You may believe love will never come again.
You may expect disappointment instead.

How Does the "Unloving Spirit" Come into Our Lives?

- when we do not follow God's Word
- down through the family line (generational)
- through abuse
- in family and/or school relationships
- through not being loved and cared for the way we should be (or, in some cases, the way we *think* we should be loved)

The unloving spirit doesn't care about our lives, whether we grew up in a poor family, or had a normal upbringing in a middle–class family, or whether our family had abundance in excess and we were given everything we ever asked for. The following testimony is about a person who had an unloving spirit and it will show how this spirit can come in and work through our lives. You will also see the connection between the unloving spirit and the *"spirit of addiction"*:

Abigail: Testimony about Unloving Spirit and Addiction

I grew up in the Church, I believed in Jesus and I gave my life to the Lord in my teens. I knew my parents both loved me, but Mom may not have known how to show it or say it. I guess I felt unloved and unappreciated by Mom. In my mind, it appeared as if I couldn't do enough to please her. Not knowing how the spirit world works, I must have agreed with the enemy that I wasn't loveable. That was an open door for the unloving spirit.

When Mom and other people talked about my little brother, I always heard how he was smarter and was so gifted. In my mind, it seemed that he got all the praise, while I got the criticism. This is a "spirit of comparison", which is a sin.

My brother had a God-given musical talent. I couldn't play a note. This opened the door for spirits of jealousy and envy.

My perception was that Mom always criticized my weight, my posture, my grades in school, etc. I had an image of being fat all my life. This brought in low self-esteem. I always had a fear of doing anything new, because I didn't think I would be able to do it, and so entered a spirit of fear – fear of the unknown.

For God has not given us the spirit of fear; but of power, and of love, and of a sound mind.
♥ *2 Timothy 1:7* NKJV

I was very sensitive and easily upset by comments made by others. It was hard for me to look people in the eye, and I didn't like what I saw in the mirror. I had a feeling of unworthiness, and the unloving spirit was reinforced in my life.

I also came from a family of drinkers. There are families that have a "familiar spirit", and trends are passed down through the family line, such as addiction, crime, molestation, abuse, etc. When I took my first drink, I liked the "buzz". I liked how it numbed my feelings and made me feel happy. It wasn't long before I looked forward to having a social drink.

When I was sixteen, I met a young man, and we dated for about three years before getting married. Dad knew his father and approved of this boy. Other guys that I brought home did not always measure up to Dad's expectations. As I look back, I know I loved him, but Dad's approval could have influenced my decision to marry him as well. That is people-pleasing, which is a trait of the unloving spirit. The unloving spirit also makes you feel that you are not good enough and no one would want to marry you.

Just before my wedding, Mom became ill but was allowed out of hospital to attend the wedding ceremony. I was thrilled that Mom could be there for me. In those days, it was a miracle that Mom had survived this type of surgery, and everyone was so happy to see her recovering so well. Perhaps, in my mind, this caused all the attention to go to Mom instead of "the beautiful bride". I felt that Mom stole some of my limelight.

We were a middle-class family, and so finances only allowed for my brother to go to university. He moved out of the country to pursue his career. I was left with all the caring for Mom. In came spirits of envy, jealousy, resentment, comparison, bitterness, and self-pity.

I was a Daddy's girl and felt that Dad loved me and made me feel special. Dad and I loved being together, laughing and doing things. Dad passed away when I was only twenty-six, and I blamed God for taking my dad from me. Dad also asked me on his deathbed to make sure I took care of Mom, and I promised I would. I loved my mom and was more than willing to take on this responsibility.

My way of coping with Dad's death was to use alcohol, and eventually drinking began to dominate my thoughts. Mom had had an illness in her childhood that affected her heart. She had two heart surgeries and a stroke in the years following Dad's death. I used alcohol to help me deal with what was happening with my mom. I guess I shunned God in my life after Dad died; I felt separated from God, and because of some other life circumstances, I started to withdraw from church. I began to use alcohol to celebrate good times, to get through bad times, to ease pain, and eventually any other excuse I could find. Alcohol became my coping mechanism.

My husband grew up in a family that did not outwardly show love, so he couldn't show his love for me, at least in the way I thought I should be loved. He also had an unloving spirit. An unloving spirit doesn't recognize love when it is shown. It can't receive it or return it. Unloving spirits keep us from initiating expressions of love. It seemed to me that I was always doing things to get my husband's approval, to feel appreciated, to get a hug or have him tell me that I was a good wife and mother or that I looked great in that dress. But he could never say it, so the unloving spirit was having a party in our lives.

When my husband left me after thirty-plus years of marriage, I drank to numb what was happening in my life. I felt rejected. Spirits of fear and panic entered in, and depression was reinforced. I felt like garbage. I didn't want to live and didn't know how I was going to go on. Just after that, Mom passed away, and I was feeling even more alone. I began to drink very heavily, and I was entertaining suicidal thoughts. I was in a pretty desperate situation, and I was very depressed, full of panic, anxiety, and fear. One day, when everything seemed to be crashing down on me and I didn't know where to turn for help, I just got down on the floor and cried out to God for help. I knew I had to choose between life and death. My whole focus went into getting free from addiction, and I started attending church again. I repented of my sins and returned to a relationship with Jesus. I was baptized and filled with the Holy Spirit. It was no longer a fight to stay away from alcohol. I believe that Jesus took that all away from me. My life began to turn around. A Christian man came into my life, and we got married. I was no longer alone.

The unloving spirit brought with him friends – spirits of unworthiness, self-pity, jealousy, envy, bitterness, rejection, and anger – into my life, but I wasn't aware of these spirits until I took the Health To You Ministry basic course called "Walking in Wholeness". Through this teaching, I was able to see how the unloving spirit had been working in my life. Through counselling and deliverance, and my faith in God, I gained my freedom, not only from the unloving spirit but from addiction to alcohol and nicotine.

Praise the Lord! I have freedom, and I am so aware that my Heavenly Father loves me just the way I am. After all, He wove me together in my mother's womb, and He doesn't make mistakes.

We are new creations in Christ! He died on the cross, defeated the devil, rose again from the dead, and lives in us today. We rejoice, knowing that because of what Jesus did for us we can be free from the past! Let's get rid of the